Brace Yourself for A Recession

A Comprehensive Guide to Protecting Your Finances, Career, and Mental Health During Economic Downturns

Author Name Sanjay Dheer

Year of Publication: 2024

Table of Contents:

Contents

Introduction:..6

Chapter 1: The Disturbing Global Situation and Coming
Recession...11

Chapter 2: How a Recession Affects Daily Life 15

Chapter 3: The Effects of recession on Financial Markets: Stocks,
Bonds, and Investments 20

Bonds: Safe Choice or Risky Option? 21

Retirement Accounts: Long-Term Effects on Savings.............22

Impact on 401(k)s, IRAs, and Pension Funds 22

Increased Pressure to Withdraw Early 23

Reduced Contributions and Employer Matching......................23

The Effect of Inflation and Interest Rates on Savings 23

The Influence on long-Term Investment Plans........................24

Methods for Safeguarding Retirement Accounts in a Recession
....25

Chapter 4: The Mental Toll of a Recession on Health and Well-
Being 26

Stress and Anxiety During a Recession...........................26

The Impact of Uncertainty..27

Impact on Family and Relationships 28

The Need for Mental Health Support and Coping Methods ...29

Chapter 5: Getting Your Finances Ready for a Recession 31

Looking for Ways to Consolidate Debt.............................33

Enhancing Savings Is Key..34

Staying Updated Is Essential..34

Chapter 6: Handling Debt Before and During a Recession..........35

Evaluating Your Debt Before a Recession................................35

Focus on High-Interest Debt 35

Evaluate Debt-to-Income Ratio..36

Paying Off High-Interest Debt 36

Consolidating Debt Before a Recession....................................37

Managing Debt During a Recession 38

Building an Emergency Fund for Debt Management................39

Chapter 7: Investing During a Recession: Risks and Opportunities
....40

Understanding Market Volatility 40

Assessing Risk Tolerance..41

Opportunities in a Downturn..41

Avoiding Common Pitfalls...42

Diversification and Staying the Course 43

Chapter 8: Keeping Your Job and Career Safe During a Recession
....44

Chapter 9: Protecting Your Business During a Recession 47

1. Assess Cash Flow and Build Reserves 47

2. Cut costs wisely...47

3. Strengthen Relationships with Customers............................48

4. Broaden Revenue Streams 49

5. Ensure Access to Credit Ahead of Time 49

6. Invest in Technology and Efficiency.....................................50

Chapter 10: Government Help and Relief in a Recession............51

Unemployment Benefits...51

Stimulus Payments...52

Food Assistance Programs..52

Rent and Mortgage Help 53

Small Business Help 53

Healthcare and Medical Help...54

Chapter 11: Getting Ready Emotionally and Mentally for a
Recession...56

Recognizing Emotional Impact.......................................56

Creating Coping Strategies 57

Chapter 12: Lessons from Past Recessions 60

Chapter 13: Strategies for Building Long-Term Financial
Resilience...63

Chapter 14: Being Financially Ready for Economic Ups and
Downs – Summary 67

Chapter 15: About the Author:...69

Introduction:

Brace Yourself for A Recession – It's Coming

In recent years, the global economy has faced increasing turbulence. From geopolitical conflicts to pandemic-induced disruptions, financial markets have been volatile, and many of the economic indicators that predict recessions are flashing red. The word "recession" tends to evoke fear and uncertainty in households and businesses alike, as memories of past economic downturns—such as the 2008 financial crisis or the COVID-19 pandemic recession—linger in our collective memory. But while recessions are indeed challenging, they are also an inevitable part of the economic cycle. And just like any challenge, the key to navigating a recession successfully lies in preparation.

To brace yourself for the next recession, it is crucial to understand what causes economic downturns, how they impact different areas of life, and, most importantly, what steps you can take to protect yourself financially and emotionally. This introduction will serve as a foundation, outlining the core themes and concerns that will be explored in this eBook, providing you with actionable insights to better prepare for what lies ahead.

What Is a Recession?

Before diving into preparation strategies, it's important to define what a recession actually is. A recession, in simple terms, is a significant decline in economic activity across an economy that lasts for an extended period—typically defined as two consecutive quarters of negative gross domestic product (GDP) growth. This contraction usually leads to a cascade of other economic issues, such as rising unemployment, shrinking consumer demand, and lower corporate profits.

The causes of a recession can vary widely. Sometimes, they are triggered by external shocks, such as the oil crisis of the 1970s or the COVID-19 pandemic, which suddenly and dramatically disrupt economic activities. In other cases, recessions are the direct result of imbalances that build up over time, such as excessive debt levels, asset bubbles, or unsustainable levels of government spending. Regardless of the cause, recessions bring widespread challenges to businesses, individuals, and governments, and their ripple effects can be long-lasting.

One common misconception about recessions is that they are rare, isolated events. In reality, recessions are part of the natural ebb and flow of the economic cycle, which alternates between periods of expansion and contraction. Economies expand as businesses invest, consumers spend, and markets thrive, but over time, these periods of growth inevitably give way to corrections. In this way, recessions act as a reset for the economy, purging inefficiencies and setting the stage for future growth.

Why Should You Care?

For the average person, it can be easy to dismiss talk of a recession as something that affects only financial markets or corporations. But the truth is that recessions have far-reaching consequences that can impact virtually every aspect of life. Job security, the value of your investments, your ability to access credit, and even your mental health can all be affected when the economy takes a downturn.

During a recession, one of the first areas to suffer is the labor market. Companies facing reduced demand for their products and services are often forced to cut costs, and this frequently results in layoffs or reduced work hours. For individuals and families, the loss of a job or a reduction in income can be devastating, especially if they are not financially prepared for such a disruption. Even those who manage to keep their jobs may find that wage growth stagnates, while the cost of living continues to rise.

In addition to the direct impact on employment, recessions often lead to a decline in asset values, which can affect anyone with investments in the stock market, real estate, or retirement accounts. For those nearing retirement, a recession can wipe out years of carefully accumulated wealth, forcing them to delay their plans or drastically reduce their lifestyle expectations. Younger individuals, too, may find it harder to get started on their financial journey, as homeownership and savings goals become more elusive during economic downturns.

Credit markets also tend to tighten during recessions. Banks and lenders become more cautious, making it more difficult for individuals and businesses to access loans or lines of credit. This can be particularly problematic for small businesses, which often rely on borrowing to maintain cash flow or fund expansions. Individuals may also find it harder to finance large purchases, such as homes or cars, or to consolidate debt at favorable interest rates.

While the financial consequences of a recession are significant, they are often compounded by the psychological toll that economic uncertainty can take. The fear of losing one's job, watching the value of investments plummet, or being unable to provide for one's family can lead to heightened levels of stress and anxiety. This emotional strain can have long-lasting effects on mental health, relationships, and overall well-being, making it essential to prepare not only financially but also mentally for the challenges ahead.

The Warning Signs of a Recession

The good news is that recessions are rarely sudden, unanticipated events. While external shocks can sometimes trigger economic downturns quickly, there are often warning signs that suggest a recession is looming. Understanding these indicators can help you take proactive steps to protect yourself before the full impact of the recession hits.

One of the most widely watched indicators of an impending recession is the behavior of the stock market. While the stock market is not the economy, it is often a leading indicator of future economic activity. When stock prices begin to decline steadily over a prolonged period, it can signal that investors are losing confidence in the future earning potential of companies, which may indicate that a recession is on the horizon.

Other key indicators include rising unemployment rates, slowing consumer spending, and declining business investment. Inflation can also play a significant role in signaling a recession. When inflation rises too quickly, it erodes purchasing power and can lead central banks to raise interest rates in an effort to cool the economy. While higher interest rates can help control inflation, they also make borrowing more expensive, which can slow down economic growth and tip the economy into recession.

Additionally, an inverted yield curve—a situation where short-term interest rates are higher than long-term rates—has historically been a reliable predictor of recessions. This occurs when investors expect economic conditions to worsen in the near term, leading them to demand higher returns for short-term investments.

Preparing for the Inevitable

Given the numerous warning signs and the cyclical nature of recessions, the question is not if a recession will occur but when. Fortunately, there are steps you can take to prepare yourself for the challenges ahead, and by doing so, you can mitigate some of the financial and emotional strain that recessions often bring.

The first step in preparing for a recession is to evaluate your financial situation. Start by building an emergency fund that can cover three to six months of living expenses. This fund will provide a cushion in case of job loss or unexpected expenses, allowing you to avoid going into debt during tough times. At the same time, focus on reducing or eliminating high-interest debt, as this can become a burden if your income declines or interest rates rise during a recession.

It's also a good idea to review your investments and consider rebalancing your portfolio to reduce exposure to high-risk assets. While it's important to stay invested for the long term, a well-diversified portfolio that includes a mix of stocks, bonds, and other assets can help you weather market volatility more effectively.

In addition to financial preparation, it's important to mentally prepare for the challenges a recession may bring. This means developing a plan to manage stress and maintain perspective during difficult times. Whether it's through meditation, exercise, or simply staying connected with friends and family, finding ways to stay grounded can help you navigate the uncertainty of a recession with greater resilience.

Chapter 1: The Disturbing Global Situation and Coming Recession

In today's connected economy, economic cycles aren't just market ups and downs—they relate closely to global events, geopolitical risks, and social changes. As we prepare for the next recession, it's important to consider the wider context of this economic downturn. While financial experts argue about when the next recession will hit, many warning signs are already visible along with growing uncertainties that might worsen economic troubles.

From the risk of new conflicts to the chance of a new pandemic, global disruptions are putting extra pressure on weak economies, raising the risk that the next recession may be worse than expected. In this chapter, we look at these global happenings, their role in economic instability, and suggestions for protecting yourself amidst this uncertainty.

The Rising Risk of War and Its Economic Effects

A major worry on the global scene today is the increasing chance of war and geopolitical conflicts. Various regions are seeing rising tensions that could lead to serious economic outcomes. A main example is the ongoing war in Ukraine, which has created major divisions between Western nations and Russia. This conflict, starting in early 2022, has resulted in widespread human suffering and disturbed global supply chains, especially in energy and food.

Europe, which heavily relies on Russian energy, is facing significant energy shortages and rising prices. Countries that used to get Russian gas have been forced to find new sources, pushing energy prices higher worldwide. For the average person, this means higher electricity bills, more expensive fuel, and inflation on basic goods. Even outside Europe, nations are feeling the impact. For instance, in the United States, climbing energy costs have driven inflation, affecting consumers and businesses alike.

The global food supply has also been impacted by the Ukraine war, as both Russia and Ukraine are key suppliers of wheat, corn, and other vital agricultural products. Disruptions in exporting these goods have led to shortages and rising prices, especially in developing countries that rely heavily on imports. This situation is causing financial strain on many households already facing inflation and low wage growth.

However, the Ukraine conflict is not the only geopolitical issue. In East Asia, tensions between China and Taiwan are climbing, raising fears of a military conflict that could disrupt trade routes globally. The South China Sea, an important trade passage, is particularly delicate. A military clash in this region could obstruct the supply of goods, especially electronics, pharmaceuticals, and raw materials crucial for manufacturers across the world. The global economy, already hurt by COVID-19 supply chain disruptions, would be further shaken by any military action there.

Another troubling area is the Middle East, where ongoing conflicts in Syria, Yemen, and now Israel and Palestine add to regional instability. This area has always been vital for the world economy due to its large oil and gas reserves. Any big increase in conflict there could lead to soaring oil prices, creating global inflationary pressures. For consumers, this means higher fuel costs, increased transportation expenses, and further inflation on goods and services.

The risk of war leads to an atmosphere of uncertainty where individuals and businesses can take steps to protect themselves. First, consumers should focus on budgeting and saving to build a financial cushion. This can help weather potential economic downturns. Second, businesses may want to reassess their supply chains and explore diversifying suppliers to mitigate risks associated with disruptions.

Additionally, companies should evaluate their financial health and consider reducing unnecessary expenses to preserve cash flow. This can enhance their resilience in tough times. Government entities should also prioritize creating flexible policies that can adapt to shifting circumstances while fostering economic growth when possible.

The potential for a recession, compounded by possible future pandemics, calls for diligence and foresight. The lessons learned from the COVID-19 pandemic highlight the importance of being prepared for unexpected economic shifts. Although the future is uncertain, taking proactive measures can help soften the blow of economic downturns, whether they arise from another health crisis or a confluence of global events. Economic instability means you should take actions to secure your financial health. This can involve creating an emergency fund, paying down debts, and having different ways to earn income so that if one source fails, you have others as backup.

It's also essential to keep updated on global news and how it might affect the economy. Watching international affairs, health issues, and economic decisions can guide you in managing your finances, investments, and career choices.

Chapter 2: How a Recession Affects Daily Life

A recession can significantly impact daily life, creating financial difficulties for individuals, families, businesses, and communities. As the economy shrinks, job losses, higher interest rates, less consumer spending, and the burden of existing debts begin to affect daily life. Understanding these effects is important because a recession's consequences reach far beyond just the financial markets; they disturb jobs, family life, and community stability.

Job Loss and Income Issues

One major and immediate effect of a recession is a rise in unemployment. As demand for goods and services drops, businesses often lay off workers to cut costs. Job cuts, hiring freezes, and reduced hours can leave many without a steady income, causing severe financial pressure. Even workers who keep their jobs might face salary reductions, smaller bonuses, or slow wage increases, complicating their ability to manage increasing living costs.

For families, losing income can be very tough. Paying for necessities like rent, food, and health services becomes hard, and saving for future goals like education and retirement may be delayed. Financial uncertainty can also increase stress at home, affecting relationships and overall health.

Higher Interest Rates and Slowed Economy

During a recession, central banks might raise interest rates to fight inflation or stabilize currency. While the goal is to control inflation, this also makes borrowing more costly. Higher interest rates mean mortgages, credit cards, and other loans become pricier to pay. Families already on tight budgets may struggle to meet the rising payments on their debts.

For businesses, increased borrowing costs can hinder access to credit, slowing growth and investments. This results in economic stagnation as firms postpone hiring, decrease production, or shut down. Small businesses particularly suffer in these situations, often relying on loans for daily operations and lacking sufficient cash reserves to survive downturns. This leads to fewer job openings and lower consumer trust, worsening the recession.

Lower Consumer Spending and Economic Activity

As job losses and rising prices affect budgets, consumers start cutting back on nonessential purchases. Sectors like retail, travel, and entertainment are hit hardest during a recession, as people prioritize saving for essentials. Declining consumer spending creates a damaging cycle: businesses see reduced income, prompting further layoffs and less investment, which slows economic growth.

Decreased spending also means families are less inclined to make major purchases, such as homes, cars, or appliances. This drop in large transactions negatively impacts important industries like real estate and construction, which drive economic activity. As companies in these fields struggle, unemployment increases, worsening the economic downturn.

Effects on Current Loans and Financial Commitments: Recessions can make it very hard for people and businesses to manage their loans and debts. When interest rates go up, monthly payments on adjustable-rate mortgages, credit cards, and variable loans can increase a lot. People already having trouble with debt may face financial ruin or foreclosure. Many families might need to sell their homes, move to smaller places, or look for financial help, which can hurt their credit scores and ability to borrow in the future.

For businesses, rising costs to service debt can reduce profits, forcing them to cut spending on investments and growth or even go bankrupt. When companies cannot meet their financial obligations, it affects the entire supply chain and local economies, leading to job losses and hurting other local businesses that depend on them.

Direct Impact on Family Life

The effects of a recession go further than just financial struggles; they can also affect the emotional state of families. Job loss or lower incomes create stress and fear at home. Parents may find it hard to provide for their children's basic needs like food and education. Sometimes, job loss and financial pressure can lead to more conflicts at home, mental health problems, and even broken relationships.

Children face problems too, as families may have to make hard choices about education and healthcare. Limited family resources can lead to fewer educational options, especially for low-income families, widening economic gaps. The mental toll of financial problems can also affect kids and teens, who feel the anxiety of their parents' struggles.

The Toll on Businesses and Communities

For businesses, recessions lead to smaller profits, decreased cash flow, and possible closure. Small and medium-sized enterprises (SMEs), which are vital to local economies, are often at greater risk. These businesses depend on consistent customers and affordable credit. When consumer spending drops and borrowing costs rise, they might have to lay off workers, cut hours, or shut down entirely. This can hurt local economies significantly, as one business closing can cause a loss of jobs and services in the community.

At the community level, the effects of a recession are clear. As businesses fail, the local economy shrinks, leading to cuts in public services, tax revenue, and quality of life. Schools, healthcare systems, and public infrastructure may have to deal with budget cuts, resulting in declining services. Lower economic activity can also increase crime rates, as those in financial trouble may resort to desperate actions. Communities with high unemployment often see lower civic engagement, as financial instability weakens social connections and increases feelings of isolation.

Local governments, tasked with providing essential services like housing assistance and healthcare, may become overwhelmed during a recession. With fewer resources, they struggle to meet the increasing demand for help, leaving vulnerable populations without the support they need. Charities and nonprofits may experience a spike in requests for aid even as their funding from donations and grants decreases.

A Collective Challenge

The impact of a recession is broad, affecting many parts of everyday life, from personal finances to community health.

Job losses, higher interest rates, less spending, and increased debt all create a cycle of financial difficulty that can be hard to break. While families, businesses, and communities feel the effects of a recession differently, the struggles are all connected thereby arising the need for teamwork to overcome the same.

During economic downturns, being ready and tough is crucial. Knowing how a recession might impact your job, family, and community can aid in making smart choices to navigate through tough times. This may include creating an emergency fund, cutting down debt, or helping local businesses. Taking such steps can lessen the harsh effects of a recession and support a smoother recovery for all.

Chapter 3: The Effects of recession on Financial Markets: Stocks, Bonds, and Investments

Recessions are well known for causing ups and downs in financial markets, deeply affecting stocks, bonds, and other investments. When the economy shrinks, financial markets usually respond quickly, causing prices to drop across many asset types. Both large and small investors experience greater uncertainty as portfolio values can fall significantly. This chapter will examine how recessions influence financial markets and investments, especially focusing on stocks, bonds, retirement funds, and savings.

Stocks: Falling Market Value and Greater Volatility

The stock market is often one of the first areas to feel recession impacts. As economic activity slows, company profits decline, causing stock prices to drop. Investors fearing more losses tend to sell their shares, leading to even lower prices, and creating a cycle that reinforces these declines. Such widespread selling results in higher market volatility, making stock markets unpredictable and susceptible to sharp changes.

During a recession, companies in nearly all industries generally experience drops in revenue and profits, which lowers their stock prices. Industries like retail, hospitality, and manufacturing are particularly hard hit as consumers reduce spending and demand for products and services falls. Even previously successful companies can see their stock prices decline as the market weakens.

For individual investors, this could lead to large losses, especially for those with heavy investments in stocks. Portfolio values may decrease quickly, leading to panic, where investors sell holdings at a loss to recover some capital. This can worsen the downward trend in stock prices, as panic selling pushes market values even lower.

Bonds: Safe Choice or Risky Option?

While stocks often struggle during recessions, bonds are typically seen as safer investments. Bonds, especially government bonds, are considered low-risk since they provide regular interest payments and return principal at maturity. In a recession, central banks often lower interest rates to help stimulate the economy, which can raise the value of existing bonds. When rates drop, the prices of bonds with higher fixed interest become more appealing to investors looking for stability in a volatile environment.

However, not all bonds escape recession impacts. Corporate bonds, especially those from firms in sectors hit hardest by the downturn, can turn into risky choices. Companies facing financial trouble may find it difficult to pay interest or might default on their bonds. This raises the risk for investors holding corporate bonds, particularly high-yield (also known as "junk") bonds that might offer greater returns but come with increased risk. In such situations, bondholders may incur losses if the issuing companies default.

For those investors who value safety, government bonds, like U.S. Treasuries, typically prove to be more dependable during a recession. They are government-backed and considered among the safest investments available. Consequently, during economic downturns, there is commonly higher demand for these government bonds. Demand for government bonds goes up, making their prices rise and yields fall. This causes investors to move money from riskier assets like stocks to the safer option of bonds.

Retirement Accounts: Long-Term Effects on Savings

Retirement accounts such as 401(k)s, IRAs, and pension funds face major impacts during recessions because they have a lot of exposure to stock markets and other investments. The worth of these retirement accounts closely depends on how financial markets perform, especially stocks, which are a big part of many retirement plans. In a recession, when stock prices drop sharply, it can cause significant losses for people saving for retirement, especially those close to retiring or who rely on market returns for their savings.

Impact on 401(k)s, IRAs, and Pension Funds

For those with 401(k)s or IRAs, a recession can be very concerning. As stock values decrease, these account balances usually fall quickly, mirroring the overall market drop. Younger workers may not feel the long-term effects as much since they have time to recover as markets often bounce back. However, those nearing retirement may face serious problems. If their retirement funds drop significantly right before they plan to retire, they might need to postpone retirement, lower their living standards, or take bigger risks to recover their losses.

Pension funds can also feel the harsh impact of a recession. These funds are typically large investors holding much stock, bonds, and other assets. When a recession hits, falling stock prices and possible corporate bond defaults can lower the value of pension fund assets. This can result in underfunded pension plans, meaning they lack enough assets to meet future obligations to retirees. In extreme situations, there might be benefit cuts or a need for government help to support the pension system.

Increased Pressure to Withdraw Early

A recession can lead to greater pressure for people to withdraw their retirement savings early. With job losses or reduced income, individuals might need to take money out from their 401(k)s or IRAs to pay immediate bills. However, early withdrawals often incur penalties and taxes, further hurting long-term savings. Additionally, selling investments during a market drop locks in losses and prevents benefiting from potential future gains when the market recovers.

Reduced Contributions and Employer Matching

During a recession, many may cut or stop funding their retirement accounts due to financial issues. While this feels necessary in the short term to keep cash flow stable, it can lead to significant long-term problems. Lower contributions mean missing out on the compounding growth that can greatly increase retirement savings over time. Furthermore, if employers cut or suspend matching contributions during hard economic times, workers miss a vital part of retirement savings.

The Effect of Inflation and Interest Rates on Savings

Inflation often rises during or after a recession, severely impacting retirement savings and purchasing power. When inflation goes up, the cost-of-living increases, decreasing the real value of retirement savings. So, even if the nominal amount in your retirement account looks stable or grows, your purchasing power might shrink, leaving you with less money for retirement needs. For retirees relying on a fixed income, inflation can drastically affect their ability to afford essential expenses. Basic needs like healthcare, shelter, and food.

Interest rates, commonly lowered in a recession, affect savings and fixed-income investments. Reduced interest rates mean that regular savings accounts and certificates of deposit (CDs) yield less, which makes it tough for people to enhance savings through interest. This situation is especially difficult for retirees who depend on interest from savings or bonds for income.

The Influence on long-Term Investment Plans

For investors focused on the long term, recessions bring both hurdles and chances. The short-term effects of a recession are usually harmful—leading to drops in portfolio values—but they also allow investments in stocks, bonds, and other assets at cheaper rates. Investors seeing the bigger picture might see market declines as a way to buy quality assets that are undervalued for a while. Historically, markets usually bounce back after recessions, and those who remain invested or buy during tough times can gain significantly when the economy improves.

Nonetheless, predicting market movements during a recession is tricky, and investors who panic and sell at the lowest points may lose out on the recovery. A steady method, such as dollar-cost averaging, where investors regularly put money in over time, can lessen the effects of market fluctuations and lead to better long-term results.

Methods for Safeguarding Retirement Accounts in a Recession

Considering the potential effects of a recession on retirement accounts and savings, it's vital for individuals to use strategies that protect their investments and ensure long-term financial stability:

1. Diversification: A diverse portfolio, incorporating various stocks, bonds, and other assets, can help minimize risk during a recession. Spreading investments across different sectors and asset categories can soften the blow of declines in any one part of the market.

2. Rebalancing: Regularly checking and adjusting your investment portfolio can ensure your asset mix aligns with your goals and risk levels. In a recession, this might mean lowering investments in high-risk stocks and raising investments in stable options like bonds.

3. Keeping Contributions Steady: Although it might feel right to cut back or halt retirement contributions in tough times, ongoing investments during a recession can yield better results over time. Buying assets when prices are down allows investors to take advantage of any market rebound.

4. Emergency Fund: A solid emergency fund can help prevent withdrawals from retirement savings during a recession. Having enough cash for three to six months of expenses can offer financial security and decrease the

necessity to use retirement accounts during economic downturns.

Chapter 4: The Mental Toll of a Recession on Health and Well-Being

A recession can greatly harm not just financial stability but also mental health. The uncertainty, job loss, financial pressure, and overall instability linked with a recession can increase levels of stress, anxiety, and depression. For many, the emotional strain of experiencing a recession is as serious as the economic issues. Understanding how a recession affects mental health is crucial, along with exploring ways to cope with and lessen these hardships.

Stress and Anxiety During a Recession

Stress and anxiety rank among the most prevalent psychological concerns during a recession. As the economy worsens, individuals confront various stressors at once: worries about job loss, diminishing savings, rising debt, and increasing living costs. This ongoing anxiety about basic needs is burdensome. Financial survival can bring stress that, if it lasts, may lead to long-term anxiety. A key stress factor during a recession is job insecurity. Worries about losing jobs, reduced hours, or pay cuts can create fear and a sense of helplessness. Even those who keep their jobs face uncertainty about the future, which can keep them on edge, worrying their financial situation could worsen. This unpredictability adds mental strain that can harm both emotional and physical well-being.

Financial strain is also a big source of stress. As incomes go down or vanish, people may find it hard to pay their bills, like rent or medical costs, and to buy everyday needs. The pressure to manage finances can feel too much, especially for those with families. Worry about financial issues can lead to sleepless nights, trouble focusing, and strained relationships, as these stresses impact daily interactions.

The Impact of Uncertainty

Uncertainty is a hallmark of a recession, and it significantly affects mental health. It becomes hard to foresee the future during economic downturns, and this uncertainty can lead to considerable discomfort. The inability to plan for tomorrow—whether for career growth, financial stability, or personal dreams—can make individuals feel powerless and discouraged.

For many, this uncertainty shows up as ongoing anxiety that hampers the ability to stay focused. People might fret about job stability, their ability to care for their families, or how to handle debts if things worsen. These worries can cause a feeling of paralysis, making it hard to act or decide due to the unpredictability of the future.

Moreover, recession-related uncertainty can diminish a person's positive outlook. Fears of the unknown paired with daily financial pressures can drain motivation and lead to despair. Lacking clear goals or security can make it tough for many to stay mentally strong, increasing vulnerability to mental health issues.

Depression and Emotional Fatigue

For some, the financial stresses of a recession can led to more serious mental health issues like depression. Job loss, financial strain, and failure to meet personal or career goals can create feelings of worthlessness and hopelessness. Losing a job can hit hard, as work often shapes a person's identity and self-worth. When that is taken away, they may feel a deep loss, leading to lower self-esteem and higher chances of depression.

Depression can worsen due to the social isolation that often comes during a recession. As people cut back on spending, they may reduce social outings or withdraw from friends and family because of shame over their financial situation. This isolation can deepen feelings of loneliness and hopelessness, making it harder for individuals to deal with emotional challenges.

Emotional exhaustion is another frequent result of long-term recession stress. Continually worrying about finances and job security can deplete emotional resources, leaving individuals feeling worn out and unable to face new challenges. This mental fatigue can hinder a person's ability to handle daily tasks and nurture relationships and work well, which adds to mental health issues.

Impact on Family and Relationships

The effects of a recession on mental health go beyond just individuals; they also impact families and relationships. Financial troubles can cause strain in marriages, partnerships, and parent-child dynamics, resulting in more arguments and stress at home. Disputes about finances, budgeting, and priorities can create gaps between family members as each person deals with pressure differently.

Parents often feel guilty or like failures if they cannot provide for their children as planned. This anxiety can lead to increased stress, which can affect how they interact with their kids. Children may sense this financial pressure, leading to their own anxiety and behavioural problems.

In some cases, money issues can result in relationship breakdowns. The emotional strain from financial problems, combined with everyday stress, can cause more conflicts, resentment, and emotional withdrawal. For couples, this can lead to separation or divorce, adding even more stress to an already tough situation.

The Need for Mental Health Support and Coping Methods

With the serious psychological effects caused by a recession, it is vital to focus on mental health during these hard times. One useful way to handle stress and anxiety is through open communication. Discussing financial worries with family, friends, or a therapist can lessen emotional burdens and provide relief. It's important to recognize that financial trouble is common during a recession, and seeking support is a constructive and healthy action.

It is also critical to develop effective coping strategies for managing the emotional fallout of a recession. Regular exercise, mindfulness, and relaxation methods can lower stress and enhance well-being. Setting small, reachable goals can help individuals regain a feeling of control and boost confidence in handling their situations.

For those facing depression, anxiety, or emotional fatigue, pursuing professional mental health support is also essential. Therapists, counsellors, and support groups can offer valuable resources for coping with tough feelings and developing resilience. Sometimes, medication may be necessary for managing serious anxiety or depression, and it is important to seek medical advice if symptoms are severe or ongoing.

Chapter 5: Getting Your Finances Ready for a Recession

To prepare for a recession, taking steps to protect finances can help avoid financial pressure and instability when the economy slows. There are important strategies individuals can use to improve their financial security before a recession strikes, helping to shield against job loss, falling investments, or rising expenses.

One key action is to build an emergency fund. This is important because job losses and income cuts are common during a recession, and having savings can cover essential expenses like rent, utilities, food, and medical bills. It is generally advised to save three to six months' worth of expenses, but more is better in uncertain economic times. For instance, during the 2008 financial crisis, many individuals who saved six months of living expenses managed to handle sudden job losses more effectively and had time to find new jobs or switch careers. Without an emergency fund, people often depend on credit, accumulate debt, or sell investments at a loss, worsening their financial situation. The aim of an emergency fund is to ensure financial stability during tough times. The purpose of a fund is to give financial safety and avoid high-interest debt when times are hard. Cutting out unnecessary costs is also a must. A recession needs a more careful way of spending where people should focus on what they need instead of what they want. This involves looking over monthly expenses and cutting back on areas like entertainment, dining, subscriptions, and luxury buys. For example, a person who spends $100 a month on streaming and $150 on eating out could use that $250 each month for savings or paying off debt. Cutting such spending releases cash that can be saved or used to create financial security. Also, prioritizing essential buys improves cash management and guarantees funds are there for key costs if income decreases.

Reviewing and changing budgets is another vital step. A clear budget is needed to track where money goes and how much is saved. Facing a possible recession, looking at your budget again helps find ways to save. For example, someone with many unneeded memberships or frequent impulse buys can use that money for paying down debts or adding to their emergency fund. When the COVID-19 pandemic struck in 2020, many had to change their budgets fast due to job loss or reduced hours. Those with flexible budgets did better managing these tough financial changes.

Paying off high-interest debt is key before a recession hits. Credit card debt and personal loans with high rates can be hard to manage when job stability is at risk. Reducing or getting rid of such debts eases the financial load during a recession when income may fall. For instance, a person with $5,000 in credit card debt at a 20% interest rate could take years to pay it off while struggling during a recession. However, if they focus on clearing the debt before a recession starts, they can use those monthly payments for more necessary costs and lower financial stress in tough times.

It's also wise to check investments and think about rebalancing. While it's not smart to completely pull out of the stock market, being overly invested in risky stocks can lead to big losses in a recession. A smart way is to balance a portfolio with safer assets, like bonds, which usually do better when markets fall. Those who mixed their investments with stocks and bonds before the 2008 recession recovered faster than those who only invested in stocks.

Even though predicting the market is hard, having a diverse investment approach can lessen losses and lessen financial ups and downs during a recession.

Another crucial step is to secure multiple income sources if possible. Relying on just one income during a recession can be risky. Building side income, whether through freelancing, part-time work, or starting a small business, can provide financial support if a main job is lost. For instance, during the 2020 economic downturn, many people with side jobs—like selling online, driving for rideshare, or freelancing—could fill the gap when they lost their main income. Having an extra income source, even if small, gives financial flexibility and lessens reliance on one pay check.

Avoiding large purchases is another key measure. Not buying expensive items like cars, luxury goods, or high-end electronics can help save cash during uncertain times. If a recession is near, holding off on these buys keeps funds free for emergencies. For example, someone thinking of getting a new car might choose to keep their old one. By lowering debt levels and increasing income where possible, individuals can bolster their financial position, making it easier to handle any downturns.

Looking for Ways to Consolidate Debt

Consolidating debts is another smart step before a recession. If someone has multiple loans or credit card debts, merging them into one lower-interest loan can ease financial pressure. For instance, a person with several high-interest credit cards might consider taking out a single personal loan with a better rate. This would not only simplify repayments but also cut down on total interest payments. Thus, they could redirect those savings toward essential costs or bolster their savings during tough times.

Enhancing Savings Is Key

Increasing savings is crucial, even if there is already an emergency fund. Adding more savings can offer additional financial security during a recession. For example, a person saving 10% of their income might choose to up that to 15% or even 20% to build a sturdier financial cushion. The more savings one has prior to a recession, the easier it is to tackle unforeseen expenses.

Staying Updated Is Essential

Additionally, staying informed about the economy is vital. By keeping an eye on economic trends and recession signs, individuals can make better financial choices. Regularly monitoring financial news, interest rate fluctuations, and job market dynamics helps one understand when to tighten spending or change financial plans.

In summary, preparing financially for a recession leads to better stability and control when economic situations worsen. By creating an emergency fund, cutting unnecessary costs, modifying budgets, and taking actionable steps like consolidating debt and diversifying income, individuals can approach a recession with more assurance and peace of mind. These steps not only safeguard financial health but also help mitigate the stress often experienced during economic downturns.

Chapter 6: Handling Debt Before and During a Recession

Debt can be troublesome, especially during tough times like a recession. In an economic downturn, job losses, income drops, and higher interest rates can create challenges in meeting loan repayments, leading to financial strain. It is essential for individuals to manage their debt proactively before a recession and know how to deal with it during challenging periods for better financial health. This chapter discusses methods for debt management both before and during a recession to alleviate worry, shield your financial future, and maintain control over your finances.

Evaluating Your Debt Before a Recession

The first thing to do for managing debt ahead of a recession is to evaluate your financial responsibilities. This means taking a close look at all open accounts, loans, credit card debts, mortgages, and other obligations. Make a list of all balances, interest rates, minimum payments, and terms for each. Knowing the full extent of your debts helps in deciding which ones to tackle first.

Focus on High-Interest Debt

High-interest debts, like credit cards and personal loans, should be addressed first. During a recession, these debts can grow quickly; even small amounts can escalate due to high interest rates. For example, a person with $10,000 in credit card debt at a 20% interest rate can see their debt balloon, especially if just making minimum payments. The priority should be to reduce or pay off these high-interest debts quickly to free up money for managing other, lower-interest loans.

Evaluate Debt-to-Income Ratio

It's also essential to look at your debt-to-income ratio, which shows what part of your monthly income is used for debt repayment. A high ratio can signal trouble, particularly during a recession when earnings might be uncertain. Cutting down this ratio before a downturn provides more financial flexibility to cope with difficulties that may arise and lessen the risk of missing payments.

Paying Off High-Interest Debt

One effective way to manage debt before a recession is to pay down high-interest debts like credit card balances and payday loans. These types of debts are costly, and during a recession, they might become hard to handle if you lose or reduce your income. By focusing on these high-interest debts before the economy declines, you can cut down on the interest you pay and have more cash for essential needs during tough times.

A common approach to paying off high-interest debt is the "debt avalanche" method. In this method, you start by paying off the debt with the highest interest rate while making minimum payments on your other debts. Once the debt with the highest interest is cleared, you move to the next one that has the second highest, and so forth. This strategy helps reduce the total interest paid and can speed up the repayment of debt. For instance, if someone has multiple credit card debts, they may start with a card that has a 25% interest rate, pay it off strongly, and then go to the next card with a 20% rate.

On the other hand, the "debt snowball" method starts with paying off the smallest debts first. This might be more motivating for people who want to see quick results since eliminating small debts early can boost confidence to tackle larger debts. Although this method may not cut down interest costs as well as the debt avalanche, it can provide motivation by reducing the number of debts outstanding.

Consolidating Debt Before a Recession

Debt consolidation can help manage several debts, especially when interest rates are high. By merging high-interest debts into one loan with a lower rate, payments can be simplified, and total interest paid can be reduced over time. For instance, consolidating credit card debt into a personal loan with a lower interest can make managing payments easier and lower monthly costs.

Before a recession, it's smart to look into debt consolidation options if you have several high-interest debts. There are various ways to consolidate debt, such as personal loans, balance transfer credit cards, or home equity loans. Each choice has advantages and disadvantages, so it's crucial to think carefully about what fits your financial needs.

A personal loan for consolidation usually offers lower rates than credit cards, and it has fixed monthly payments, which helps with budgeting. Balance transfer credit cards might give 0% interest for a limited time, allowing debt to be paid off without extra interest. However, these cards often come with transfer fees and may revert to high rates after the promotional period. Home equity loans or lines of credit can also help consolidate debt, but they can risk losing your home if payments are missed, making them a more dangerous choice.

Managing Debt During a Recession

When a recession begins, managing debt may be harder, especially if your income is less or unexpected costs arise. The first thing to do during a recession is to keep making minimum payments on all debts to protect your credit score and avoid late fees. If possible, keep paying more than the minimum on high-interest debts to stop them from increasing.

If making payments is hard, it's vital to contact creditors right away. Many lenders offer hardship programs or loan changes during economic downturns, which may provide temporary relief through lower payments, delayed payments, or reduced interest rates. For instance, during the COVID-19 recession, many mortgage lenders created forbearance programs letting homeowners pause payments without going into default foreclosure. By talking to creditors early, you can negotiate better terms and prevent falling behind on payments.

Also, when interest rates fall during a recession, think about refinancing your loans. Refinancing might reduce your monthly payments by getting a lower interest rate, particularly for bigger loans like mortgages or car loans. However, you must consider refinancing costs, such as closing fees, against potential savings to make sure it's a good decision for you.

During a recession, it is vital to avoid new debt unless it is absolutely necessary. New loans or credit card debts can increase your financial strain, especially with high interest rates or unstable income. Concentrate on managing your current debt and decreasing it if you can, instead of taking on more debt.

Building an Emergency Fund for Debt Management

An emergency fund is key to managing debt in a recession. With some savings, you can avoid using credit cards or loans for unexpected expenses like medical bills, car repairs, or temporary job loss. If you haven't started an emergency fund, begin by saving money as soon as you can. Aim for three to six months' worth of living costs to help you if you lose a job or earn less.

An emergency fund can help you not default on debt during a recession, which protects your credit score and prevents extra interest and fees. By using your savings for necessary expenses, you can keep to your debt repayment plan even when facing financial issues.

Chapter 7: Investing During a Recession: Risks and Opportunities

Investing in a recession might feel strange. As markets drop and the economy struggles, many investors worry, about selling assets and sticking to cash or low-risk investments. However, a recession has risks but also offers chances for smart investors who can keep a long-term view. Knowing how to handle investment challenges during economic downturns is key for protecting wealth and getting ready for future profits when the economy improves.

Understanding Market Volatility

A recession usually causes significant ups and downs in financial markets. Stock prices may quickly fall as companies see their sales and profits drop, while consumer spending decreases and unemployment rises. In these times, investors often feel fear and uncertainty, wanting to exit the market to avoid more losses.

But, it's vital to understand that volatility is normal in investing. Markets have cycles, and downturns are often followed by recoveries. For instance, during the 2008 financial crisis, the stock market dropped sharply, causing panic. Yet, those who stayed in or bought more shares during low points gained significantly when the market recovered in the following years. History indicates that downturns, while difficult, do not last forever, and markets eventually recover.

Assessing Risk Tolerance

Before making any investment choices during a recession, it's important to evaluate your risk tolerance. Some investors feel at ease with market fluctuations and are willing to keep or even boost investments in riskier assets, while others may want to shift to safer options. Your risk tolerance is influenced by various factors, including your timeline, financial objectives, and comfort with market changes.

For younger investors with a long timeline, continuing to invest in stocks during recession can be wise. They have a chance to wait out market swings and can gain from buying stocks at lower prices. For example, a 25-year-old investing in a diversified portfolio... A portfolio of stocks during a downturn may see some growth in the next few decades when the market gets better. For those close to retirement or with less time to invest, a safer approach may be needed. It's crucial to keep investing, but these individuals might want to adjust their portfolios to include more bonds or other stable assets to lessen risk and safeguard their savings against big losses.

Opportunities in a Downturn

One key opportunity during a recession is buying stocks at lower prices. When the economy shrinks, stock values usually go down as companies show lower profits and investor trust fades. For people with a long-term focus, this can be a good time to buy solid companies stocks at reduced prices. Stocks that seemed too high-priced in boom times might become cheaper, leading to potential big gains when the market improves.

For instance, during the COVID-19 downturn in early 2020, many well-known stocks dropped sharply. Investors who bought shares of firms like Apple, Microsoft, or Amazon at their low points saw their investments grow significantly when the market bounced back later in the year. Historically, bear markets, where stocks drop by 20% or more, often offer the best chances for long-term investors who are patient and smart.

Another chance involves stocks that pay dividends. During a recession, companies with strong finances and steady income usually keep paying dividends to their shareholders, even if their stock prices fall. Investing in dividend stocks during a downturn can provide a regular income while waiting for stock prices to rise again. These companies are generally more stable and better able to withstand tough economic conditions.

Bonds, especially government ones, can also be a safe option in a recession. As central banks often reduce interest rates to boost the economy, the value of existing bonds with higher rates increases, making them a good investment. Bonds provide fixed returns, helping to stabilize a portfolio during uncertain times. Investors seeking to lower their risk during a recession may think about moving some of their investments into bonds to safeguard their capital and earn income.

Avoiding Common Pitfalls

Though there are chances during a recession, several common mistakes should be avoided. One of the most harmful is panic selling. When markets drop, it's natural to want to cut losses and exit. However, selling at the market's lowest point locks in losses and stops you from benefiting from the eventual recovery. In the 2008 financial crisis, many investors who sold their stocks at the lowest missed out on the significant gains that followed.

Another mistake is attempting to time the market. It's nearly impossible to predict when the market will hit its lowest point or when it will begin to recover. Investors who wait for the "ideal" moment to invest often miss significant opportunities. Instead of trying to time the market, a smarter strategy is to keep investing regularly through dollar-cost averaging. This means investing a set amount of money at regular intervals, regardless of market situations. Over time, this method helps to balance out market fluctuations and minimizes the risk of poor timing.

Diversification and Staying the Course

Diversifying is essential for managing risk during a recession. By spreading investments across various asset types, sectors, and regions, you can lower the effects of a downturn in any one area in your overall portfolio. For instance, while retail and hospitality stocks may struggle during a recession, sectors like healthcare and consumer staples tend to be steadier. By spreading out your investments, you make sure your portfolio balances risk and stability.

Finally, sticking to your plan is very important for investing in a recession. It might be easy to react to quick market changes, but good investing needs patience. Recessions won't last forever, and the market will bounce back eventually. By following a solid investment plan, investing regularly, and not making emotional choices, you can come out of the recession in a better financial state.

Chapter 8: Keeping Your Job and Career Safe During a Recession

A recession can hurt job security a lot since companies often lay off workers to save money. It's vital to take action to secure your job and career during tough economic periods. By making yourself a key employee, improving your skills, and exploring different career paths, you can boost your chances of staying hired or finding new work if necessary.

The first thing you should do to keep your job is to show that you are valuable to your employer. It's crucial to show how you can help the company make money. Take on extra tasks, suggest solutions to issues, and volunteer for projects that are beyond your usual duties. Employees who are seen as providing value are less likely to be laid off. Employers Favor workers who contribute to the company's success, especially when things are tough.

Another smart idea is to network at your workplace. Building good connections with coworkers and supervisors can make you more noticeable and better linked. Networking allows you to stay updated on what's going on in the company and helps you manage any changes. Good relationships with management can also lead to better chances of keeping your job during layoffs. If they trust you, they might advocate for your position. Regular communication and teamwork create chances to show your worth.

Learning new skills and pursuing education are vital for job security. Industries change quickly, especially in recessions when companies seek flexible employees. Think about getting professional certificates, taking online classes, or attending workshops relevant to your industry. Knowing the latest trends or gaining new skills will give you an advantage. Employees who don't grow are at higher risk, while those who can adapt are more valued.

Also, enhancing your soft skills is equally necessary. Skills like leadership, communication, problem-solving, and adaptability increase your value as an employee. For instance, being able to lead in a crisis or stay calm under pressure is something employers appreciate. Improving these skills helps you deal with challenges during a recession.

Establishing a personal brand in your field can also protect your career. By positioning yourself as an expert through writing, public speaking, or engaging on platforms like LinkedIn, you increase your visibility to future employers. A strong professional image means that even if your job is at risk, you have a better chance of finding new opportunities. Companies and people known for their expertise often receive offers more frequently.

Another key tactic during a recession is to diversify your income. Depending solely on one income source can be risky when job security is shaky. Freelancing, consulting, or launching a side business can help shield your finances if your main job is uncertain. For instance, many professionals who might face job losses, layoffs during a recession are encouraged to start a side hustle for passive income generation. However, it must be done thoughtfully. Start by evaluating all business expenses to identify non-essential costs that can be trimmed without harming productivity. Avoid making cuts that could negatively impact customer service or employee morale. Instead, look at options like renegotiating contracts with suppliers, reducing discretionary spending, or implementing energy-saving measures.

Chapter 9: Protecting Your Business During a Recession

A recession presents significant challenges for businesses of all sizes. Reduced consumer spending, tighter access to credit, and overall economic uncertainty can lead to declining revenue and rising operational difficulties. However, with careful planning and strategic adjustments, businesses can not only survive but potentially emerge stronger once the economy recovers. Here are key strategies to protect your business during a recession.

1. Assess Cash Flow and Build Reserves

Cash flow is the lifeblood of any business, especially during a recession when sales may decrease, and customers take longer to pay. The first step in protecting your business is to assess and understand your current cash flow situation. Regularly reviewing financial statements, cash flow forecasts, and outstanding invoices will give you a clear picture of your liquidity. This enables you to identify potential cash flow shortfalls before they become critical.

Building a cash reserve is also essential. If possible, set aside extra funds to cover essential operating costs, such as payroll, rent, and utilities, for several months. Having a cash cushion allows you to weather short-term revenue declines and unexpected expenses without needing to take on high-interest debt or make drastic cuts.

2. Cut costs wisely

Reducing costs is a necessary step in recession-proofing your business. However, it's important to make thoughtful cuts rather than slashing expenses indiscriminately. Start by identifying non-essential or low-priority expenses that can be reduced or eliminated. This may include delaying new equipment purchases, reducing discretionary spending on travel or events, and negotiating better terms with suppliers.

While it may be tempting to cut marketing budgets during tough times, this can be a mistake. Businesses that continue to invest in marketing during a recession often gain market share as competitors scale back. Instead of cutting marketing completely, consider shifting to lower-cost channels such as social media or email marketing, which can maintain your brand presence while conserving funds.

Similarly, avoid cutting key staff or skilled workers unless absolutely necessary. Layoffs can lead to operational disruptions, reduced morale, and loss of institutional knowledge. If your business needs to reduce labor costs, consider alternatives such as reducing hours, offering unpaid leave, or freezing new hires.

3. Strengthen Relationships with Customers

Maintaining strong relationships with your customers is crucial during a recession. Customers are more selective with their spending during economic downturns, and businesses need to work harder to retain loyalty. Focus on providing exceptional customer service and value, even if it means adjusting your pricing or terms to better meet customer's needs.

Consider offering flexible payment options, such as instalment plans or extended payment terms, to help customers manage their finances. You can also introduce promotions or discounts to encourage repeat business, but be careful not to undermine your brand's value by discounting too aggressively.

Listen to customer feedback and adapt your offerings to meet changing demands. If you notice shifts in customer preferences or behaviours due to the recession, be flexible and adjust your product or service mix accordingly. For example, during the 2008 recession, many companies in the retail and service industries pivoted to more affordable options or bundled services to accommodate reduced consumer spending.

4. Broaden Revenue Streams

Depending too much on one product, service, or market can make your business more exposed during a recession. To guard against falling revenue, seek ways to broaden your offerings and enter new markets. For example, if your main product is seeing a drop in demand, think about adding other services that could bring in more money.

Many businesses change direction during a recession by growing their online presence or starting new lines of business. E-commerce grew a lot during the COVID-19 pandemic, as many physical stores launched websites to reach wider audiences. Likewise, service providers can look into offering online consultations or digital products to support in-person services.

Expanding your customer base can also help protect your business from local economic issues or sector slowdowns. If you mainly operate in one area, think about opportunities to grow into nearby regions or even international markets.

5. Ensure Access to Credit Ahead of Time

Getting credit can be harder during a recession as banks tighten lending and interest rates change. To avoid being left without financial help, secure lines of credit or loans before cash flow issues arise. Creating a good connection with your bank or financial institution when your business is doing well can help you get better terms.

If you think you'll need credit during a recession, apply for it early. Waiting until your business is in trouble can make it harder to get loans or may result in worse borrowing conditions.

Consider exploring loans from government or relief programs for small businesses, which often increase during bad economic times.

6. Invest in Technology and Efficiency

Even though a recession might not seem like a good time for new investments, updating technology and working on efficiency can help keep your business competitive and lower costs in the long run. Automating routine tasks, improving your supply chain, and investing in software to make operations smoother can increase productivity without adding more staff.

Also, using data analysis to follow important performance indicators (KPIs) and customer patterns can help you make better decisions. Companies that focus on efficiency during a recession are generally in a stronger position to grow quickly when the economy gets better.

Chapter 10: Government Help and Relief in a Recession

In a recession, governments are key in assisting people, families, and businesses handle the tough economic times. Government programs can offer financial help, prevent widespread poverty, and lessen the worst impacts of a recession. In this chapter, we will look at different types of government support usually available during economic downturns, how these programs operate, and how to access them when necessary.

Unemployment Benefits

A common type of government support during a recession is unemployment benefits. When individuals lose jobs due to company cutbacks, closures, or other economic reasons, these benefits provide temporary financial help. They cover basic living costs like housing, food, and utilities while people look for new jobs.

In most countries, these benefits are funded by taxes and differ in amount based on the person's previous income and the length of unemployment. For example, in the U.S., benefits are based on a percentage of a person's prior earnings, up to a cap. During the COVID-19 pandemic, extra federal benefits were provided, increasing the weekly amount and extending the benefits duration to assist those affected by mass job losses.

Applying for these benefits usually has a simple process. People need to show proof of job loss and past income, and sometimes they may need to actively seek a new job while getting benefits. Governments often change the amount and time frame of benefits during a recession to help more people, as seen in the 2008 financial crisis and the 2020 pandemic.

Stimulus Payments

Governments may send direct payments to individuals and families during a recession to help stimulate economic activity and give quick financial relief. These are often called stimulus checks and aim to quickly provide money to consumers, encouraging spending to lift demand for goods and services. The goal is to increase spending so businesses benefit and the economy stabilizes faster.

For instance, in 2020, the U.S. issued several rounds of stimulus checks to individuals as part of the response to COVID-19. These payments provided essential support for millions of Americans who lost jobs or faced income reduction. The funds were typically distributed through direct deposit, checks, or debit cards, making it efficient and easy to access.

While these payments offer immediate help, they are normally one-off or short-term solutions. Hence, recipients should think carefully about how to use the money, prioritizing essential expenses like rent, bills, or reducing debt, rather than treating it as extra income.

Food Assistance Programs

Food insecurity tends to increase during a recession as many people and families find it hard to manage their budgets. To combat this, many governments expand access to food assistance programs during economic downturns. These programs give money help or food support to aid low-income people and families get healthy meals.

In the United States, the Supplemental Nutrition Assistance Program (SNAP), also known as food stamps, is the main food assistance. SNAP benefits come with an Electronic Benefit Transfer (EBT) card that users can use to buy food. In downturns, SNAP eligibility rules are often made easier, and benefit amounts can go up so more people can get food.

Other regions have similar programs, like the UK's Healthy Start vouchers, which help pregnant women and families with young kids buy healthy food. Food banks and community groups also help by giving free food to those in need.

Rent and Mortgage Help

Housing security often gets at risk in a recession as people lose jobs or earn less money. Governments usually start rent and mortgage help programs to stop evictions and foreclosures. This help can be direct money aid for rent or mortgage, or legal protections to stop landlords from evicting or banks from foreclosing during the downturn.

For instance, during the COVID-19 crisis, many governments set up eviction bans, stopping landlords from evicting renters who couldn't pay. Likewise, mortgage pause programs allowed homeowners to stop or cut mortgage payments without risk of losing their homes. These programs gave families time to recover from the downturn impacts.

Applying for rent or mortgage help usually means showing money troubles from the recession, like losing a job or big income drops. Governments might also team up with non-profit groups and housing services to provide these programs and extra support, like legal aid for tenants facing eviction.

Small Business Help

Recessions can hit small businesses hard since they often have low profits and little cash saved. To aid small businesses in these hard times, governments often offer help programs like grants, low-interest loans, and tax relief.

For example, in response to the COVID-19 crisis, the U.S. government launched the Pay check Protection Program (PPP), which gave forgivable loans to small businesses for payroll, rent, and utility costs. Various countries also cut business taxes or postponed tax payments to help small business owners manage money flow and prevent bankruptcy during hard times.

Getting small business help usually means applying through government offices, local banks, or financial institutions. The application process often needs proof of the business's money situation, including revenue loss due to the downturn and how the relief funds will be used. Eligible small businesses can use the funds to keep staff, cover operating costs, or invest in new ways to make money.

Healthcare and Medical Help

In a recession, getting affordable healthcare can be a big problem for many people and families, especially those who lose their jobs and health insurance from work. In response, governments often widen healthcare coverage or start short-term programs to make sure people can access medical services during tough times.

In the United States, programs like Medicaid provide healthcare for low-income individuals and families. During recessions, Medicaid eligibility rules may be relaxed to let more people qualify for care. Likewise, lots of countries with national healthcare systems... increase money to make sure that people without jobs or with low-paying jobs can still get medical help without too much cost. Also, governments may provide temporary aid for healthcare payments or give free COVID-19 testing and treatment during a pandemic. Access to mental health resources, which often struggle during hard economic times, is also widened to assist people in dealing with the emotional impacts of financial issues.

Chapter 11: Getting Ready Emotionally and Mentally for a Recession

The emotional and mental challenges of a recession can be as tough as the financial ones. Economic downturns create uncertainty, worry, and pressure as individuals and families face job loss, reduced savings, and changing economic conditions. Preparing emotionally and mentally for a recession is vital for staying strong, handling stress, and focusing on future goals. By creating coping methods, keeping perspective, and centering on mental health, you can address the emotional difficulties of a recession with more steadiness.

Recognizing Emotional Impact

Recessions usually lead to increased stress and worry. The dread of job loss, watching savings shrink, or having trouble paying bills can cause a lot of emotional strain. For many, financial issues lead to feelings of powerlessness and a lack of control, which can worsen mental health conditions like depression, anxiety, or ongoing stress. Even those who still have jobs or are financially stable may feel anxiety because of the unpredictability ahead and the difficulties faced by those around them.

Not knowing how long the recession will last or if one's finances will be affected is tough to deal with and can cause emotional pain. This lack of certainty can make individuals feel overwhelmed, hindering clear thinking and wise decision-making.

Realizing these emotional reactions is the first step in mentally preparing for a recession. Acknowledging that stress and anxiety are common responses to uncertainty and financial strain can help lessen stigma and form a basis for constructively addressing these feelings.

Creating Coping Strategies

One effective method to handle the emotional challenges of a recession is to develop coping strategies that support mental health. These methods can help reduce stress and anxiety and offer a feeling of control during chaotic times.

1. Build a Support System

Having a good support system of friends, family, and coworkers can greatly help during a recession. Talking about your worries, addressing financial hurdles, and seeking guidance from trusted people can reduce feelings of loneliness. A supportive circle can provide both practical help and emotional support, helping you keep perspective during hard times. Don't hesitate to ask for help, whether it's chatting with a friend or consulting a financial expert.

2. Stay Informed, But Don't Overload

It's important to know what is happening in the economy, but constantly taking in recession-related news can increase anxiety. Limit your exposure to upsetting news and choose your information sources wisely. Look for trustworthy and balanced news outlets, and avoid spending too much time on negative stories or dramatic reporting. Set a routine for checking financial updates, focusing on actions you can take instead of worrying about the overall economy.

3. Use Stress-Reduction Techniques

Techniques like mindfulness, meditation, and relaxation can help manage stress effectively. Activities such as deep breathing, yoga, or even short meditation sessions can help you stay calm during anxious moments. Regular physical activity can also support your mental well-being. activity decreases stress and helps clear the mind. Simple walks or brief workouts can improve your mood and how you deal with stress.

4. Control What You Can

Recessions can make many feel like they have no power, especially with worries about job safety or money. To feel more in control, concentrate on what you can change in your life. This could mean making a budget, cutting back on unneeded spending, or saving for emergencies. Taking small, clear steps to improve your finances can help boost your confidence and lessen anxiety.

5. Set Achievable Goals

It's key to know that recessions can bring financial troubles, but it's just as crucial to have realistic goals during this time. Recognize that you might need to change your financial aims, delay big purchases, or adjust your daily life for a while. Accepting these shifts as part of a bigger economic pattern can help manage your disappointment and frustration better.

6. Taking Care of Mental Health

Keeping good mental health during a recession needs constant care and attention. Financial pressures can heavily impact your emotional state, so it's vital to focus on self-care and consider professional support if necessary.

If stress, anxiety, or depression feel too much, think about talking to a therapist. Mental health experts can share ways to deal with emotional issues, and many offer affordable or remote help. Seeking support for mental health is a proactive approach to prepare for the psychological challenges of a recession.

Keeping routines and focusing on well-being is another way to protect your mental state. Eating well, sleeping enough, staying active, and keeping social connections are key to emotional strength. Focusing on these habits during tough times can provide a sense of stability and continuity, even with unpredictable outside factors.

Chapter 12: Lessons from Past Recessions

Recessions are not new. Economies have gone up and down throughout history, sometimes in big ways. Each recession is different, but there are useful lessons from past downturns. From the Great Depression in the 1930s to the 2008 crisis and the COVID-19 recession in 2020, these events show patterns in human behavior, money management, and the strength of those who were prepared. By reflecting on these incidents, we can gain insights to face future issues with assurance.

The Great Depression: Value of Flexibility

The Great Depression of the 1930s is one of the worst economic crises in modern times. Millions lost jobs, homes, and money quickly. The 1929 stock market crash caused widespread fear, but the long economic slump taught many lasting lessons.

A key lesson from the Great Depression is the need for flexibility. As businesses failed, those who adapted—through learning new skills or changing jobs—did better. My grandfather lived through this time as a farmer, but when farming suffered, he began repairing farm tools to provide for his family. It wasn't fancy, but it helped him keep food on the table.

In tough economic times, being adaptable can save you. Whether it's learning new skills, changing fields, or starting side jobs, the ability to adjust to new situations can be very important. If there's one takeaway from that generation's experience, it's that being inflexible in hard times can be detrimental. Change can cause more difficulties, but being adaptable can create new chances.

The 2008 Financial Crisis: The Risks of Over-Leverage

The 2008 financial crisis is fresh in the minds of many. It was when housing markets failed, banks collapsed, and millions lost jobs and homes. The crisis highlighted the risks of being over-leveraged, affecting both individuals and institutions. Before the crash, many bought homes they could not pay for, took loans without fully understanding them, or invested in risky financial products. When the bubble burst, the results were severe.

I recall a friend who purchased a house in 2006 with an adjustable-rate mortgage, believing real estate would guarantee wealth. Like others, he did not fully understand the risks. When his mortgage payments increased two years later due to interest rate changes, he couldn't keep up. In the end, he lost his house and had to restart, both financially and emotionally.

The key lesson is the need for financial caution. Steering clear of over-leverage—whether in loans, credit, or risky investments—can protect you from harsh outcomes during economic slumps. Knowing the terms of your financial agreements and living within your means can shield you from negative impacts when markets shift unfavourably.

The COVID-19 Recession: The Importance of Emergency Funds

The COVID-19 pandemic led to an unusual recession. Suddenly, businesses shuttered, millions lost jobs, and the global economy stopped. The pandemic showcased how fragile economies can be and why having an emergency fund is crucial.

When the pandemic struck, those who had saved for emergencies fared much better in facing the economic shock. I remember talking to a former coworker who had saved enough for three to six months of expenses. Although she lost her job, her emergency fund allowed her the time to secure new employment without the panic of affording rent or groceries. In contrast, many others I knew had to incur credit card debt or ask friends and family for money just to survive.

The lesson from the COVID-19 recession is straightforward: having an emergency fund is vital. While experts have long advised saving for emergencies, this period proved just how important it is. Economic downturns can come unexpectedly, and having a financial cushion can be the difference between managing well and struggling under pressure.

Patterns of Resilience: Lessons Learned

Several recurring themes emerge from these recessions. First, preparation matters. Having savings, avoiding risky investments, or being flexible helps those better prepared to handle tough times. Second, resilience often stems from mindset as much as from financial stability. Those who embraced change, kept a positive attitude, and were proactive tended to recover faster.

Despite economic struggles, human resilience stands out. Lessons from past recessions teach us that we can prepare ourselves both financially and mentally for hard times. By learning from history, we can confront future recessions with a strategy—remaining adaptable, living within our means, and saving for unforeseen difficulties. Every recession can be a chance to grow stronger, both as individuals and communities. It's not only about evading hardships; it's about knowing how to endure and emerge better from them.

Chapter 13: Strategies for Building Long-Term Financial Resilience

Creating long-term financial resilience is critical for handling the unavoidable ups and downs of life, especially during economic downturns like recessions. Financial resilience means more than just having savings—it includes managing debt carefully, developing diverse sources of income, and maintaining a flexible mindset. By taking a forward-thinking approach to personal finances, you can create a solid base that can handle emergencies and provide financial safety for the future.

1. Build a Strong Emergency Fund

A key step in gaining financial strength is to set up a strong emergency fund. This fund should cover at least three to six months of living costs, including rent or mortgage, bills, food, and other necessities. An emergency fund serves as a safety net during job loss, health issues, or unforeseen costs.

I once had a friend who, during the 2020 pandemic, lost his job without warning. Luckily, he had saved enough to cover six months of expenses. Although he was stressed, he could concentrate on job hunting without worrying about bills. His emergency fund allowed him time to recover. This example highlights the value of emergency savings—not just for financial survival but also for peace of mind.

2. Diversify Your Income Sources

Depending on one income source can leave you financially weak. To build financial strength, create multiple income sources to help you through tough times. This could be through side jobs, freelance work, or investments, adding security to your finances.

For instance, a colleague works full-time as a graphic designer while taking on freelance projects. When layoffs happened during an economic slump, she leaned on her freelance work for income. Her diversified earnings not only softened the blow of her job loss but also opened new job prospects. This shows the importance of not relying on one income source if you can build more.

3. Cut and Manage Debt

Having a lot of debt can make you financially unstable, especially in hard economic times. A key component of financial strength is to cut high-interest debt, like credit card debt, and handle other debts wisely. Reducing debt means you can save and invest more, leading to long-term stability.

A family member prioritized paying off credit card debt after college. Instead of spending extra money, she focused on cutting her debt and following a budget. Years later, when a recession hit, she had no high-interest debts and could stay financially stable while others faced challenges. Smart debt management eases short-term financial stress and puts you in a better place during economic downturns.

4. Invest in Your Skills and Knowledge

Skills and education are key assets. Investing in your education and personal growth keeps you competitive in the job market, especially during tough economic times. Ongoing learning makes you adaptable to shifts in industries and job needs.

For example, a software engineer took data science courses during a slow career phase. When his company downsized during a recession, he was able to transition to a sought-after data science role. His commitment to education kept him relevant in a tough job market, showing that skill development is essential for lasting financial strength.

5. Create a Long-Term Investment Plan

Investing is an important way to grow wealth over time and boost financial strength. However, having a diversified investment strategy is crucial to align with your risk tolerance and financial targets. Spreading your money around different types of investments—like stocks, bonds, real estate, and even things like peer-to-peer lending—can help reduce risk.

Imagine a person who started putting money into index funds in their 20s, contributing a bit each month. Over the years, their investments grew, not due to big market jumps, but because they stuck to a steady, long-term plan. When tough times hit, their diverse investments helped them manage well, and they kept investing, even when others left the market in worry. This shows how important it is to stay committed to investments and aim for long-term growth instead of responding to short-term market changes.

6. Live Within Your Means

It is easier to build financial stability when you spend less than you make. By saving more, consistently investing, and avoiding debt, you create a solid foundation. Many people grow their wealth by focusing on saving and making smart choices instead of spending excessively.

For example, a coworker makes a decent salary but drives an older car and does not buy flashy things. He focuses on saving and investing, which has led him to build a significant savings over time. When economic issues arise, he feels secure because his lifestyle fits his income, allowing him to adjust to different financial situations.

Chapter 14: Being Financially Ready for Economic Ups and Downs – Summary

The book serves as a detailed guide to dealing with economic uncertainty and preparing for downturns. Its main points include:

• Recognizing global economic complexities and spotting early signals of a recession, like stock market trends and central bank actions.

• Understanding how recessions affect life, such as job losses and rising interest rates, with strategies for managing debts and spending.

• Analysing the effects of recessions on financial markets, including stocks, bonds, and other investments.

• Discussing the mental effects of recessions and offering ways to manage stress and worry.

• Important steps to prep finances before a recession, like creating an emergency fund and reducing costs.

• Guidance on handling debt wisely and making smart investments during tough times.

• Advice on safeguarding your job and business when the economy takes a hit.

• Information on government assistance and relief available during recessions.

• Stressing the importance of mental and emotional readiness for hard economic times.

• Sharing lessons from past recessions to guide future actions.

• Concluding with methods to create long-term financial strength, including saving, diversifying income, and debt management.

Being financially ready for economic uncertainty involves active financial management, mental toughness, and a long-term view. By using the lessons from each chapter, you can protect your finances, adjust to changing economic conditions, and succeed through whatever challenges come your way. With careful planning and perseverance, you can face the future with assurance, prepared for whatever lies ahead.

Chapter 15: About the Author:

Sanjay Dheer is a renowned international marketing expert with a distinguished career spanning over two decades. Holding a Master's degree from a prestigious business school, he has successfully navigated diverse global markets, establishing himself as a trusted authority in the field.

Having travelled to over 88 countries, Dheer has gained profound insights into various cultural and business landscapes. His professional journey has taken him to key hubs such as Hong Kong, Dubai, Bahrain, and Seattle, where he has driven growth and innovation for leading organizations.

Recognized for his strategic acumen, Dheer's ability to blend cultural understanding with marketing expertise has made him a sought-after consultant for industry leaders aiming to expand their global reach. His work not only reflects his commitment to excellence but also his passion for fostering cross-cultural connections in business.

In addition to his professional achievements, Sanjay Dheer enjoys sharing his insights through writing and empowering others to succeed in the ever-evolving world of international marketing.

Thank You Note

Dear Reader,

Thank you sincerely for choosing *Brace Yourself for Recession: A Comprehensive Guide to Protecting Your Finances, Career, and Mental Health During Economic Downturns*

I'm deeply grateful that you've decided to explore this book, especially in times when preparing for economic challenges is more crucial than ever. Writing this was both a mission and a passion, and I hope that it equips you with practical tools, knowledge, and encouragement to navigate and even thrive through turbulent times.

If you found the book insightful, I would be honored if you could leave a review on Amazon or Goodreads. Your thoughts not only help other readers find the book but also inspire me to continue creating resources that make a difference.

For ongoing updates, articles, and insights, please feel free to connect with me on LinkedIn or follow me on Instagram.

I'd love to stay in touch and hear how you're preparing to brace for the future.

With gratitude,
Sanjay Dheer

Other Books by the Author:

**Sustainable Investing:** Investing for a Better Tomorrow: A Comprehensive Guide to Green Investing

Create Wealth, Not Money: Wealth Creation: A Proven Framework

**Neuroscience of Creativity: Unlocking the Secrets of the Brain:** Dive into the science of creativity, how the brain fosters innovation, and ways to tap into hidden creative potential.

(Coming Soon)

Thank You

www.ingramcontent.com/pod-product-compliance
Lightning Source LLC
Chambersburg PA
CBHW070124230526
45472CB00004B/1414